Hundred and Fifty Four Sonnets

CONTENTS

FOREWORD xiii

Sonnet for Chris 1
I Wept 2
Cholitas Climb 3
Richard Gere 4
Old Lady 5
Crying 6
The Masanafu Boys 7
Influencer 8
Every Breath 9
Driftwood Lady 10
A Fleeting Fragrance 11
Trust 12
The Girls 13
Is the Law an Ass? 14
Crazy Ride 15
Things 16

	Art and Law	17
	Harper Left Alice Springs	18
	A Little More Cripple Each Day	19
	No Place/Time to Breathe	20
	The Freedom Worth Wanting	21
	Backache Again	22
	Analytical Idealism	23
	I Have No Clue	24
	Words Unplugged	25
	An idea	26
	They Don't Regret It	27
	Backache 3	28
	Little Sister	29
	Alice Springs	30
	PhD Research	31
	The Bees' Knees	32
	How "The Elephant's Tooth" Came About	33
	A Balancing Act	34
	University of Newcastle	35
	No Desires	36
	Dance and Sing	37
	Free Will and Mens Rea	38
	I Like What I Do, Thank You	39

People!	40
Japanese Designer	41
When we Are Discovered	42
Perfect Days	43
Mother Japan	44
Erica	45
Simpson Desert	46
A Shitty Day	47
Bleep	48
Teaching a Horse to Sing	49
No Regrets	50
I Wish	51
Dear Japan	52
Powerless Rebellious Acts	53
Marks on Paper	54
The Yellow Rabbit	55
Centrelink	56
No Face	57
Mushrooms	58
A Strange Request	59
On The River of Time: Just Compassion	60
That Little Church	61
Shapeshifters	62

That Point, That Moment	63
The Post	64
We Are Asymmetrical	65
My Mother and Red Current	66
Singing	67
A Three Dog Day	68
Ex	69
Retirement	70
Exactly What I Want	71
Rothko Exhibition	72
Puppets	73
How Adults Talk to Babies	74
Simpson Desert	75
Phoning Faye	76
Old Male Friends	77
Short-Circuited	78
Aristotle's Riddle	79
How God Travelled	80
The Lime Tree	81
The Ghan Departs	82
She is Something Else	83
Retired!	84
Quick, Call the Priest!	85
Love is Blind	86

| When Feeling Triggered 87
| Thing-Flings 88
| The Dance the Body Remembers 89
| Dance with the Cold 90
| Dancing the Red Line 91
| Performance in Brussels 1983 92
| Gravity 93
| Rabbit Hole 94
| At Home in the World 95
| Bob 96
| Today 97
| You and Me 98
| What Rests 99
| In Spirit 100
| Indian Winter 101
| One Bitter Line 102
| The Key of Me 103
| Merci 104
| What is Real? 105
| Arigatou! 106
| Köszönöm! 107
| The Cold Press Juicer 108
| Chez Nous 109
| Me 110

Japanese Potato Salad 111
Coffee with a Layer of Cream 112
Like Bread So Sweet 113
Suddenly 114
Morning Routine 115
Millions of Little Universes 116
My Mum's Chicory Salad 117
Poor Mailboxes 118
Peeling Broad Beans 119
Second Childhood 120
Things That Make You Rich 121
The Not-Seen 122
Unknowable 123
Whatever My Eye Can See 124
To Seek Refuge by Thyself 125
The Scorn of Yuletide 126
Anti-natalism 127
Old Men and Books 128
Not Long Anymore 129
Modern Medicine 130
Stuff 131
Freedom 132
Tooth Elf 133
Reminder 134

Today 135
Marianne 136
Barack Obama 137
The Cottage 138
Japanese Poetry 139
Election Angst 140
Olive Pink Botanical Garden 141
Bed Rotting 142
Ichi-go Ichi 143
Remember 144
Dark Night 145
Rapture 146
After the Backache 147
Mother 148
Sister Drunk on the Floor 149
Sonnet With an Extra Word at the End 150
Witlof 151
The First Seconds 152
They've Gone Away 153
Hundred And Fifty-Four Sonnets 154

ABOUT SONNETS 155
ABOUT THE AUTHOR 159
LEGAL PAGE 163

Hundred and Fifty Four Sonnets

Suzanne Visser

FOREWORD

A sonnet is like a little explosion. First, there is the idea. Such an idea arrives in my mind from the outside, like a text message. Ping. There it is. When thoughts begin to stream and mingle around the idea, I must be quick and catch them in lines. These lines then must rhyme: ABABCDCDEFEFGG. Ideally, there are ten syllables per line, not counting silent ones.

I am caught in a little time bubble universe while writing a sonnet. I must grab all that is given at that very moment.

Before I wrote this series of sonnets, One Hundred and Fifty-Four Sonnets, I had never written a sonnet. The first sonnet in this bundle was the second sonnet I ever wrote. The second sonnet I ever wrote is the first sonnet in this bundle. Then Chris asked me why I like sonnets. I explained in an email: I just like sonnets. There's something comforting about them. They spring to mind easily. I explained in a sonnet:

> I don't know where they come from these sonnets
> They appear through me rather than from me
> Their onset is on planets and comets
> Among trees and in the depths of the seas

I decided to write hundred and fifty-four sonnets, just like Shakespeare. I wrote a sonnet a day and put them one by one on my Facebook page, where they were liked or loved or even cared for by a small group of regulars. Thank you, Yoko, Beatriz, Heather, Lily, Mark, Rolf, Bronwyn, Katarina, Haydn, Scott, Kerrie, Pamela, Pat, Faye, Phil, Majella, Hein.... for an international and diverse audience.

Hundred and fifty-four days later, I wrote the last sonnet of this bundle. Whether it will be my very last sonnet indeed remains to be seen. Have the sonnets improved over these hundred and fifty-four days of practice, or have they gotten worse? Or did they remain of the same quality? What do their graphs look like? How do they fluctuate? It is for the reader to find out and judge.

Suzanne Visser
October 2024

Sonnet for Chris

I don't know where they come from these sonnets
They appear through me rather than from me
Their onset is on planets and comets
Among trees and in the depths of the seas
Taken with a grain of salt and a wink
They are meant to be modern and funny
They are not the replacement of a shrink
Nor quite Shakespearean either, honey
They may come from Goddess herself, who knows?
A message from the Muse for the masses
It is she who makes them live, grow, and glow
I am the mere flute through which it all passes
They are not flawless, but they are honest
And if you don't like them, blame the goddess!

I Wept

How cruelly I was torn from eternity
Pushed into stink and bitter sharp edges
From timeless peace into stark modernity
Thrown down tiny before worldly judges
They did not like me and put me into glass
They did not quite know what they were doing
Under their spotlight, a role I did cast
Their needs the stage for endless pursuing
Damn, they expected the impossible
They did not realise what they had done
Their wishes were far beyond the typical
A course set in motion, the damage began
Brutally into my life I was swept
All I foresaw and I bitterly wept

Cholitas Climb

I wept when I stumbled upon a film
About native women in Bolivia
Who, with top hats on and in layered skirts
Fly to far away, alien Argentina
For climbing a mountain to its summit
They've never been away from home before
and pray to the angry mountain spirit
The freedom from their husbands they adore
They dance with climbers, strangers in the night
In the kitchen of base camp number three
Baring their golden teeth and ample arms
With hearts so light, their spirits free
At the top they plant a flag for freedom
Shy but proud; seen at last, a little stardom

Richard Gere

I smiled when I suddenly encountered
Richard Gere driving a BMW
His hair brushed back, his dark eyes wandered
The latest model, the hotter, mind you
The older he gets, the better he looks
The deeper he stares into a woman's eyes
And with his abrupt man-movements he hooks
Any woman, while a little she cries
If anyone would ask me what is the most
beautiful thing you've ever encountered
I would answer today without a doubt
"How Richard Gere's right eye wandered"
Stormy nights at the beach of Rodanthe
In the BMW, is what I fancy

Old Lady

Now I am the thick lady whom I so
despised when I was young and stupid
Her thin skin, her wrinkles, her sparrow bones
The dread that I remember so vivid
It's surprisingly better than I thought
A mildness has descended on my mind
A fluffy bird watching what old age brought
A wild white dove near my ear to remind
Remind me of dumb errors I've made
Of crucial mistakes never undone
They fade away while I too slowly fade
With nowhere to hide and nowhere to run
Oh, this dark and wounded heart will return
to its source, where it will burn, and unlearn

Crying

I cry, it is a sign that I'm alive
From birth I've been weeping, sobbing, bawling
Wailing, whimpering makes that I survive
Blubbering, snivelling, yelping, howling....
Not only great sadness makes me tearful
Full of mourning, lamenting, sorrowing
Great beauty too makes me so damn cheerful
That I begin yowling, snuffling, squealing...
Music, paintings, poetry, you name it
It makes me whine, blub, ululate, lament
I blame it on these objects that omit
A scent from the wee thing they represent
A thing that is not of this world and can't
be named and is there only to enchant

The Masanafu Boys

These two mad, beautiful boys of colour
Appear from wrecked cars or ruined buildings
Carrying old, broken stuff. They're brothers
Wearing odd shoes, dancing and lip-syncing
Old, spattered paint rollers their microphone
They lip-sync Boney M's, 'Daddy Cool'
Using a ladle as their saxophone
They lip-sync: 'She is crazy like a fool'
They swing their hips: 'She was the meanest cat'
They moonwalk well, 'in old Chicago town'
Pants inside out: 'She left her husband flat'
Croc on one foot: 'She really mowed them down'
'Ma Baker', now one is wearing a dress
'Ma Baker', a recipe for success!

Influencer

Have you noticed: the best influencers
Have a very simple message: they wok
a spectacular meal, or they mentor
how to tie a shawl, a knot, or buy stock
As an influencer unintended
Founder of Alice Springs' Bulletin Board
With twenty thousand eager commentators
I need strong moderation skills, my lord!
People can be snakes on the World Wide Web
Their decent communication skills die
Instead, like a rash, nasty wrong words spread
Quick like wildfire, making everyone sigh
There's only one remedy against it
Ban stupid crooks for life to prevent it

https://www.facebook.com/groups/2628915324031092

Every Breath

It's good to learn young that everyone
you know disappears from your life sooner
or later. I repeat: e-ve-ry-one
you cared for, I'm not some tasteless crooner
It is the damned truth, and it causes pain
I've tried antinatalism but that's
like being against God, storm, sun, or rain
while we're losing our grandmums and our cat
Then the occasional friend of a friend
Then the real true friend, my God who is next?
It is not happening, we still pretend
We deny it, we are stunned, perplexed
It is not morbid to think about death
It makes you grateful for every breath

Driftwood Lady

I lived my life like a piece of driftwood
Swept out to sea in a terrible storm
Only so the falsehood was understood
That I could reform, transform, or perform
It is never too early to learn that
Nothing is under control, yours or mine
Praise or blame: that we don't at all earn that
Everything is up to something divine
What I thought I wanted I never got
But what I got became what I wanted
It took a while to understand that knot
Something entirely else was granted
The storm has not ceased, I'm not yet done
But sometimes I wish I was… bloop! Gone

A Fleeting Fragrance

I sometimes smell a light, fleeting fragrance
So nice, I long to have it back all week
I sniff around to reveal its agent
But can't find its source, it is just too weak
Like a sniffing machine or dog I go
Mourning the perfume I have just mislaid
Barely there and tender like fresh snow
The adorable aroma just played
a trick on me, a vile vanishing act
And I give up, thinking I have dreamed it
But then, there it is again the exact
same bouquet, who or what the hell sent it?
It must come from somewhere extremely neat
Someplace where things are sweet, right, and complete

Trust

Our Gus deserves to wear a tuxedo
A top hat on his head and a cravat
The way he escorts me to my door, bro
Along the meandering garden path
He's enthusiastic when home I return
Greets me at the gate like a gentleman
Ev'ry day again, he shows his concern
Gus, our perfectly lovely doorman
Sometimes he jumps like a jolly dolphin
Sometimes he walks like an overstuffed bear
Or saunters, stumbling ever so often
But always with the most wonderful care
As you may have gathered by now, Gus is
our dog, our Stafford, who knows what trust is

The Girls

The girls were pretty annoying today
One shrieked, another pecked me on the shin
No, the pen was not quite peaceful today
Long wrinkled necks and beaks reached for my skin
I went around with the sunflower seeds
Put some greens down for the restless ladies
The spoiled-rotten queens, they sped to their feed
Being actually horrible bullies
But from their feathery annoying bums
Fall nuts generally known as eh... eggs
They are too many, that's why they become
Scum, they need some strict policies and regs
They have gone to sleep now on messy nests
I hope tomorrow they'll be at their bests

Is the Law an Ass?

The law calms me down and at the same time
makes me feel strange'ly alert and alive
I'm not talking law & order versus crime
But about justice, that illusive drive
in women mostly, to end suffering
Lady Justice alone against the tide
of crimes committed by men unknowing
of their feminine side, war-tender pride
like a large pregnant jennet the law is
heavy and slow, sometimes blind with old pain
She carves a path to the ancient abyss
of human strain and conflict about gain
I sit on her back, and I hold her mane
She gallops me to a place that seems sane

Crazy Ride

Well, well, well, it has been a crazy ride
Hasn't it? Nothing went as it was due
No sextant, no map, no compass, no guide
The weather was vile, and I had no clue
Blinded I sailed 'round the blackened sea
Through waves of darkness, I navigated
Now 'n then a jewel lighted up: Maarten
The children, but we got separated
The weather was ter'ble and I was weak
No equipment was e'er given to me
Nobody helped me. Why? I was unique
Such is the mad curse of my family
I've done not too bad, but I am sad that
Through it all, I never had a comrade

Things

Things! They don't stick to me, they just depart
Eager for the next owner, or they leave
They break or disappear or blow apart
Bereave me as I watch in disbelief
How the microwave dies after a month
How the bottom falls out of a plant pot
Legs of a chair break, disappearing socks...
A friend's crazy about my polkadot
dress. Here, have it, I have no use for it
She eyes my orange shoes too, but I'll hang
onto those a little longer, they fit
Until Gus' teeth get a hold of them, dang!
Then, when the sharp pang of departing pain
lessens, I sigh. The opposite of gain

Art and Law

When everything has been done and tried
and nothing was soothing, or helped, or worked
When all my enthusiasm had long died
I turned to the arts and got enveloped
Art never failed to return to the light
that bored, broken, difficult heart of mine
To where excitement lives, delight and might
Where refinement and the divine combine
into a spell-bounding, mesmerising blend
of recognition, surprise, bliss and awe
Art is truly a reliable friend
And lately (surprise) also: the law
I came young to the arts, late to the law
Now they are both there as a final straw

Harper Left Alice Springs

She is too earnest for her age, the way
her brow furrows, her bobby haircut sways
Serious, lost in thought and far away
She walks up to me on a summer's day
And I feel the pain she so young endured
She's much better now, but never the same
Part of her youth gone, but cured, she matured
And found, like I did, that words were her flame
Sipping coffee in the shade at Yaye
We always talk about the written word
Saturdays, always at the same cafe
She: dark, young, I: white, old, we compared notes
for a couple of years, then suddenly
Harper packed up and moved back to Sydney

A Little More Cripple Each Day

Did you ever imagine in Japan
When you visited me in Amsterdam
That one day, we would email each other
About daily medications, brother
We better get a grip, but truth be said
We also talk about music and art
and exes and coffee and our own death
It does not matter that we are apart
A kind of far'way spouse you became
A spouse *sans* the power game or the blame
A synthetic daily bud to exchange
A whole range of stuff from art to no-change
As we became a little more crippled
Each day, the number of emails tripled

No Place/Time to Breathe

When I do not focus on anything
And just live my life like a cat or dog
I very quickly become unhinged
And pestered by random thoughts and brain fog
I must always have a project or four
Preferably for the long term, thick books
PhD research, a business, and more
While also looking after thirteen chooks
If/when the amount of pressure lessens
my mind starts having sessions of random
dumb obsessions, impressions, expressions
Phantoms I cannot seem to abandon
I cannot stand'em and need to find fast
Now! Immediately! A project that lasts

The Freedom Worth Wanting

After concentrating, I truly need
A distraction and write a quick sonnet
I need to cease reading and now proceed
To write another sonnet, I'm on it
It is compulsion rather than pleasure
As if I'm called by a whispering voice:
"Maybe this time it will be a treasure"
So, you cannot really call it a choice
Speaking of which, I believe that free will
to do anything is an illusion
a bitter pill that perhaps may instil
the tendency to follow delusions
So, sonnets deserve neither praise nor blame
They're just farts by something without a name

Backache Again

I hate to move, but I used to love it
Chris cannot move and says it is pure hell
Still at least, I can sense my own bullshit
And smell again that strange illusive smell
That fleeting fragrance that seems to appear
from utter'ly nowhere, I can't move now
for the fear of it to yet disappear
But no, there it is again: wow wow wow
I better start moving or I will shrink
Till nothing is left, not a wee muscle
I may already be on the sheer brink
Of becoming a shellfish, a mussel
I fantasise all will be well & Zen
And I will dance, run, skip, and jump again

Analytical Idealism

There is a tendency in science now
To think of the universe building blocks
As made of mind instead of matter. How?
(And this may well knock you off your wee socks)
It makes the hard problem of consciousness fade
And not only that, unbeliev'bly so
The small and the large worlds to co-relate
Experience as origin, you know
It sure does make sense, as in 'elegance'
Instead of rock-hard determinism
Which does not seem to exactly enhance
A sense of ease, but causes fatalism
Analytical idealism
Seems to instil a sense of optimism

I Have No Clue

I am a well that never stops brimming
I write faster than my readers can cope
At times like these I seem to be singing
In a higher mind state brought on by dope
A soft voice is dictating from the void
And I better have my keyboard ready
Or it will get cloyed and bloody annoyed
Who is he/she? A child? An entity?
Or is it an 'it' that relentlessly
Knocks on my doors of higher perception
Tireless, reckless, careless, fearless, restless
And while I am utterly defenceless
Puts words in my fingers and in my mouth
I have no clue as to what it's about

Words Unplugged

I call endless brimming words: an 'unplug'
As word fall, others follow like gunshots
Like pearls, machine gun bullets that were stuck
On their string by a knot now undone, shots
previously stopped by a safety pin
Words now glide free like poop from a loose gut
And begin to swim, combine, dance and spin
Like pearls bouncing off the floor, or bullets
off a steel door or matrix avatars
Words are too jumpy, a bit like cullets
they behave a little like fire or stars
uncontrollable like icy droplets
Ah, you cannot catch words with your fingers
You've got to tame them, the little swingers

An idea

I had an idea before I began
Delivered to my brain like a letter
But then the mostly unused doorbell rang
Its chime shattered my thoughts light as feathers
The words I had framed began to disband
The rhythm on my mind started to falter
Clumsily, I grasped for the thread at hand
Hoping the Muse's word wouldn't alter
Returning, I found my paper quite blank
My vision, once clear, now a foggy mess
I wrote something down, though my spirits sank
Each word was a struggle, each line a guess
But through the chaos, a new idea grew
Forming a sonnet both vibrant and true

They Don't Regret It

They say that the world is going to shit
That go-getters win, and their abettors
But I don't think it's true; I don't see it
I think the world is getting better
What parents did to kids when I was young
is rightly seen as criminal today
But back then they thought it was simply fun
Sex 'n drugs 'n rock 'n roll on display
Smoked, drank, took drugs like there's no tomorrow
Kids in the back seat of the Citroën
Narcissists, hedonists to the marrow
And they would do it all over again
The summer of love, Woodstock, the drama
It took a lifetime to shed the trauma

Backache 3

For forty years, I've had pain in my back
I tell my spine every day it is fine
I'm tired of it and want to give it back
To whomev'r made the faulty design
It's long out of warranty, so I'll pay
A brand-new golden exo-skeleton
Will do the trick so I can again play
Dance, jump, skip, swing or run a Marathon
Don't ever advise me *your* show pony
Your herb tea is not going to mend me
Nor is your cacao ceremony
Or your aroma voodoo baloney
I want comfort; am tired and cranky
To cry into, hand me that old hanky

Little Sister

She finally spoke to me, Lisette
My one and only little fulblood sis
Long lost, sassy, funny, cute brunette
Wish I could give her a sisterly kiss
Oh, she was lovely when we were children
But when we grew older, she turned away
She did not see what I was shouldering
She listened to gossip, chin-wag, three-way
Her 'sorry' came fast and was genuine
Moved, I accepted her apology
A new sistership about to begin
(we share biology, psychology)
For the sake of our children, she wanted
To cast out the things that us both haunted

Alice Springs

She is the red beating heart of the land
down under. She is battered and sunburned
Build with red clay on red rock and red sand
Many have left her, and many returned
to this mysterious and ancient heart
That beats in synchronicity with mine
It is hard to be apart, or depart
from her blue skies, her warmth, and her sunshine
I miss her already before I've left
She pulls at me with invisible strings
I miss her already, my heart bereft
The rivers just call and the soil just clings
Community, art, the church, books, these things
Forever bound am I by Alice Springs

PhD Research

PhD research: self-inflicted pain
Above anything else the candidate
must keep supervisors happy and sane
Candidates must fully participate
in endless red pen edits, many rounds
in which their text and ideas are butchered
Several versions of chapters abound
The whole study constantly restructured
One supervisor gainsays the other
The candidate tries to jump through both hoops
And they still contradict one another
The candidate bravely recoups
In short: It's hell, torment, horror, the pits
And I love every minute of it

The Bees' Knees

There are three hives under the pepper tree
Where thousands of bees reside with their queens
They work or buzz around the garden free
Their architecture within wooden screens
is endlessly fascinating and cool
meand'ring tunnels dripping with honey
extracted in white with a special tool
while smoke rises and the gold is runny
When the wax is placed in a centrifuge
Large pots are filled with the liquid gold
While the restless bees try to find refuge
In the process hundreds of flowers are polled
The honey is fragrant and delicious
Light amber, aromatic, scrumptious

How "The Elephant's Tooth" Came About

Faceless zombies began attacking me
Making my work 'bout race identity
Cancelled by a woke ethics committee
I scorn Charles Darwin University
Somewhere in the middle of my degree
They chose to ruthlessly cancel me
Students were not told their identity
They were convinced of their divinity
Their woke dribble was truly appalling
Meaningful research was made impossible
Pretending to "assist", they came crawling
The damage they did irreversible
I called them "the Gestapo" and forsook
CDU; I published my work as a book

A Balancing Act

A day without a sonnet is not good
My brain misses the thrill of the puzzle
The pieces a theme not yet understood
But at the surface, ready to sizzle
An idea lands as light as a feather
It needs to be seen and recognised first
It needs interpretation, like the weather
Then expression, like in a soap bells' burst
It needs to stay in line and not escape
its boundaries much, or it will tumble
Too much freedom will sure wreck its shape
Too much form will make it stumble
The right amount of lead should be given
By intuition it should be driven

University of Newcastle

After being cancelled at CDU
I moved to Newcastle University
I did not give up, but quickly regrouped
To research justice's sustainability
UON law school is quite a haven
CDU is crude and vulgar compared
CDU was hell, UON heaven
My trust in academia repaired
I move through my doctorate quite slickly
Gently guided by intelligent minds
I am writing my thesis quite quickly
Trying to not break my scope's confines
A PhD is the most difficult
thing one can do, we don't know the result

No Desires

I found one million seventy-nine thousand
one hundred dollars in the trunk of a tree
Fountains of hundred-dollar bills, mountains!
Enough for a two-year long shopping spree
The problem is where to safely stash
it if one cannot take it to the bank
and one cannot. It needs to remain cash
Am I a thief now? No? Who do I thank?
The problem is that I don't need a thing
I was content before the find occurred
by chance. I don't like cars; I don't like bling
The whole situation is rather absurd
It causes many moral dilemmas
That can only be solved by math's lemmas

Dance and Sing

I like serenity, immobility
Stillness in a chair is my goal in life
The whole day I practice rigidity
I bend like an old Swiss army knife
Come and dance with me in rigidity
The dance of two steps back, one step forwards
Celebrate my immovability
with me. Rejoice in stasis afterwards
I like indolence, inactivity
I am quiet and idle like a stone
I adore sluggishness and apathy
So, sing with me from head to toe:
Everyone likes the hustle and bustle
But I like to not move a single muscle

Free Will and Mens Rea

We think we have free will 'cause we *feel* it
Magically somewhere along the line
of neurons building, the brain reveals it
free will in humans by magic design
Our entire moral and legal landscapes
built upon this feeling-based fallacy
for the mere sake to finally escape
true human intentions and responsibility
How wrong we have been and how wrong we are
Is shown by hard-assed deterministic science
This whole god, soul, mind, ego, self bazaar
Has derailed our reliance, compliance
The mind is a giant billiard table
Where trillions of balls able, disable…

I Like What I Do, Thank You

I love the silence of being alone
The serenity of true solitude
The calm quietness of a stone
Being removed from multitude
I love being uncommunicative
Muteness, yes, it suits me right to the core
The absence of any collaborative
Peaceful stillness is what I most adore
Come, get out into the sunshine, they say
Let's cycle and swim and do gymnastics
However, I say: Hey, but who are they
To tell me what should be my characteristics
I don't tell them: Hey, get off your high horse
Write a book, or a poem or study a course

People!

This pretentious blow-in Italian place
Thinks it brings culture to this Outback town
Their customer service is a disgrace
An overpriced attitude from this clown
Leaves unsuspecting clients bewildered
I've never ever seen something like it
I tried to have some food home-delivered
This caused a customer disservice fit
The food was bad, too much money was paid
The place deserves an enormous phallus
You wonder how the place can even trade
The name of the joint is *Bella Alice*
I now need an ayahuasca retreat
Reset and make sure to never repeat

Japanese Designer

Being old means to a few women 'luck'
A woman becomes invisible, so
she does no longer give a single fuck
No longer follows that hollow shadow
of what others think of her façade
Zero. Zip. Nix. Nada. Null. Nil, Zilch
She wears pearls and socks in sandals
While driving a beat Toyota HiAce
Her designer a seven-year-old boy
Who wears sunglasses and dresses in black
The cutest and sweetest sight to behold
He is from Japan, with his turtleneck
He chose her cool paint-spattered orange shoes
His name is Aarush and he is her Muse

When we Are Discovered

The simplicity and glory of a
warm winter's day. The sky so ripe and blue
People nearby are laughing. I'd love
to know what with. The world feels fresh and new
Maybe they too suddenly feel that awe
for this soft dome that seems to cover us
Vaguely there is a scent of fresh straw
It would be great if God discovered us
li'l ants with consciousness going about
their day, suddenly, simultaneously
discover that this very moment out
is all we have, so ingeniously
so harmoniously, spontaneously
so graciously, so curiously, so free....

Perfect Days

The most perfect movie is Perfect Days
By Wim Wenders, the story of stories
The film of films deserving endless praise
It tells the tales of the minor glories
Koji Yakusho cleans Tokyo toilets
Eighties music in the car on cassettes
Tokyo's roads while the player uncoils it
Millions of shops & houses' silhouettes
Min Tanaka dances the homeless guy
Trees photographed or taken as bonzai
Shadows on buildings and patches of sky
Tears. Sumida Gawa. The shadow guy...
Ima wa Ima! Kondo wa kondo! Bow.
Ah, later is later and now is now!

Mother Japan

After watching Perfect Days: days, weeks, months
This deep, safe, warm, sense of Mother Japan
mixed with the sadness of not belonging
Of *mura hachibu* from the clan, man
They can make you feel the outcast *gaijin*
The baby torn from the nurturing breast
The one with the different eyes and skin
Never a member but always a guest
She is cruel and tender, lighthearted
and dark. She gives generously, but takes
away easy. Left me brokenhearted
and longing for her thund'ring earthquakes
Oh, Mother Japan, how to not grieve you
Every Perfect Day since I left you

Erica

Erica has left us, quick and gentle
We talked, she dined, she slept, she fell, she went
I'm trying not to be sentimental
She was ninety years and felt rather spent
But waves of grief assault me on day one
I knew her only briefly but intense
She was someone fierce and sharp, then was none
Went from bones and skin contained to immense
From one breath to the other she was gone
a gentle flame in the wind, feather light
There's nothing we could have done, she was done
Bright winter's night, like a kite she took flight
Unwavering she went to her maker
Leaving her shell to the undertaker

Simpson Desert

In my swag I watch how the stars travel
along the night sky, not caring at all
whether we live, thrive, die, or unravel
a passing morning cloud makes me feel small
it continues on its way, not giving
 a flying fuck about what lays below
the almost dead, the dead, and the living
until an uncaring pregnant wind blows
it away and scatters it across the sky
looking down on us like one big blue eye
watching our suffering, uncaring and dry
while a haughty and arrogant sun fries
my hat, while I step on tiny beings
who have towards me similar feelings

A Shitty Day

They are rare and far apart: shitty days
Today is the day! A pretty shitty day!
A grey day. Tax time resulting in pay
A mood that does not allow any play
A headache from dessert dehydration
A back pain that requires medication
Conflicting thoughts demand mediation
Generally, a shitty vibration
It is too cold, too dry, too wintery
Uni's compulsory unit: "Consent"
The unit's contents rather slippery
There is no way to be simply content
How do I escape this matrix of doom
Nothing on Netflix either, just the gloom...

Bleep

What is life but a brief interruption
in the eternal peace of nothingness?
A period of senseless consumption
in an endless ocean of emptiness
A burst of experience, thought, feeling
through a surface otherwise calm and still
A phase of plots, knots, conflict and healing
accumulating in eternal chill
A deep sigh, a laugh, a whisper, a scream
to the moon, planets, stars and to the sun
A beam that gleams in a violent dream
from which we will wake up when we are done
A torrent of odours, colours and sound
against an infinite timeless background

Teaching a Horse to Sing

It's always nice to see Johnno again
for coffee and a chat at Olive Pink
He always manages to entertain
And tells Persian stories while we drink:
Horse thief steals horse from the Shah of Persia
He gets caught and the Shah says: 'Give me one
good damn reason why my militia
should not shoot you with a gun for fun'
'I'll teach your horse to sing', the thief exclaims
'Okay', says the Shah. 'I give you a year'
The thief's friend says: 'You idiot! Explain!'
'Well', says the thief, 'I have got a whole year....
In which the Shah may die, or I, or something...
The horse may die or even learn to sing...'

No Regrets

I'd rather end up wishing I hadn't
than wishing I had and be maddened
rather than, like so many, saddened
My sins are so predictably patterned
stemming from childhood and Mummy and Dad
A devilish couple from Narcissi
Lead me to initially be mad, bad…
Paved the way of impending alchemy
and then the eternal quest to break free
finally, from leaden shackles and chains
to a future which was not yet the enemy
Archetypical tale of loss and gain
I'd rather end up wishing I hadn't
than wishing I had. And so, no regrets!

I Wish

Oh, I wish I had wishes, but I don't
Ah, Contentment Now is my middle name
I wish I knew when that began, but don't
The consumer in me has died, I claim
What would instil in me the flame of need
has left the building silent as a thief
Left it abandoned surrounded by weed
and trees that drop multi-coloured leaves
I make art but I hardly consume it
There are too many artists, art is reduced
to craft at best and well, the rest of it
things, possessions, stuff, gear, objects used
Best are matters made of wind, sky, sea, trees
Clouds, blood, sand... hardly worth a shopping spree

Dear Japan

Japan, Japan why did I e'er leave you?
Jesus Christ, Japan, I left you for a man!
What would I be when I had not left you?
Would I hate you or love you, my Japan?
Cozy and safe, you still instil in me
a warm glow, after all these lands and years
I still dream of you ev'ry night, you see
Japan, you still have me in longing tears
I have found another place that I love
But nothing compares to you, my Japan
You are the secret undying beloved
Japan, more worthy of love than a man
ever can be. You have been through so much
pain since I left you. Your besotted Dutch

Powerless Rebellious Acts

I used to run away from home in socks
Defeat came quickly when my socks got wet
Crying, I had to fumble with the locks
Furious with either Mum or Dad
As a teen I threw my clothes around
And stamped on them to show everyone
how wounded I was, and I somehow found
satisfaction in such a deed. No one
cared of course. I found protest in the street
against the bomb and against pollution
Yelling at policemen, earned me a seat
For three hours in juvenile detention
Old now, I pipe whipped cream into my mouth
Oh shame! Straight from the spray can, when I pout

Marks on Paper

I draw gum leaves and culms too of bamboo
And landscape-like undulating bodies
Paper: hemp fibre with hibiscus glue
Sepia inks: little to no body
My brushes are made of twigs and some shit
a rag, a bunch of hairs, a piece of mop
My pens: old, dried bamboo culm that is split
All I need is a flat smooth tabletop
The studio: the last place where bodies
are so sacred and not sexualised
Respected and not mere commodities
Form and light and shadow idealised
It is important to exaggerate
To emancipate and celebrate

The Yellow Rabbit

The court house's yellow rabbit sculpture
As example of local corruption
As insult to local arts and culture
Is in for a bit of reconstruction
Nobody knows it's meaning, relevance
maker, approver, or its audience
The bunny totally lacks eloquence
A flat yellow Miffy sans elegance
Maybe made by the maladroit nephew
of a shitty local politician
an art school rookie with no clue
The thing needs a bit of a beautician
So, let's turn the whole doe around tonight
bend its ears, paint its lips before midnight

Centrelink

Ah, applying for the old age pension
Should be a breeze, a dignified matter
Instead, it's apprehension and tension
An exercise causing the brain shatter
Hours of listening to queue muzak
followed by confusing conversations
with untrained morons who only talk back
and try to adjust your expectations
then transfer you to another number
where the queue and the muzak start anew
turning your brain into a cucumber
explain again until your face is blue
While that road gets rougher and tougher
It's designed to make older folks suffer

No Face

When you point straight at your face (try it)
And ask yourself: what am I pointing at?
You most probably find after a bit
of observing from a 1st person's view, that
you're not pointing at a face but a void
A place that is unborn and undying
Note*: To make assumptions you must avoid
When you see a 3rd person you're lying
When you find that void you can clearly see
That you are bottomless and oh so vast
Completely transparent, don't you agree?
In that void there is no future or past
You *are* that wide open space, that no-face
that no-time, no-place, no-space: That grace

Mushrooms

Within seconds, my view engulfed by smoke
Space fractured into thousand hexagons
and shattered. No time to regret the dope
Sucked into a black hole, I faced the dragons
I ceased to exist: no ego, no self
no memories, dreams, hopes or fears
everything was stripped away from the self:
Woman, animal, spirit disappeared
What only can be described as an "IT"
Didn't want, expect, think, remember, dread
anything. But it experienced. Did
it ever! There was no space and no death
a timeless universe, terror there was
blended with ecstasy, it simply was

A Strange Request

Let me lie to you, lie to you, spin you
a yarn. Let me lie to you, deceive you
Pull the wool over your eyes, lie to you
Oh, let me bend the truth and lie to you
You may ask me why I would lie to you
Ah telling tall tales and lead you astray
Fabricate stories that are far from true
'Well, just for the heck of it,' I would say
Let me just lie to you, just for one day
Because it excites me to lie to you
Be dishonest, a con artist, a stray
Falsify, bluff, fib, and mislead you
Let me hoodwink, deceive, feign and invent
Perjure under oath, dupe, distort, pretend...
Lailala Lailala Lie
Lailala Lailala Lie
Etc....

On The River of Time: Just Compassion

On the river of time with my fellow
animals, plants, trees, fungi, rocks, and mounts....
Creatures that chirp, cry, roar, sing, talk, bellow....
There is only one thing that truly counts
On the river of time drifts everything
in one direction. Share on that river
air and oar and raft, really anything
Lungs, livers, brains, and hearts quiver and shiver
In unison, all one organism
on the river of time, on one vessel
we wander away from altruism
towards conflict and struggle and wrestle
reactivity, distraction and fraction
Just compassion can bring satisfaction

That Little Church

That little brick church of my childhood years
In a sleepy village of barns and farms
My aunt played the organ, I was in tears
My grandfather's strong arms the church bell rang
My grandmother cleaned spiderwebs away
from the dark high rafters on Saturdays
The tall windows let in coloured sun rays
In echoed song, grandmother gave praise
Later, the Church of Satan rented it
And painted its majestic doors violet
Its tall brick tower toppled down from it
Someone made a B&B out of it
In the small graveyard my grandparents rest
Writing this down gives me pain in my chest

Shapeshifters

Shapeshifters have traumatic childhoods
I'm one of them, I'm two of them
Shapeshifters are like a tree in the woods
I'm three of them, I'm four of them
Deep into the earth, high into the sky
They feel. They feel everything. They feel all.
They see trees when they open their eyes
are part of the forest until they fall
Falling, they sigh, falling, they cry, they lie
They are the multitudes, they are many
You will meet a different one each time
Before you know it, you have met twenty
From dumb as fuck to pretty much sublime
Shapeshifters are powerful but tragic

That Point, That Moment

When will come that point where the future will
become the enemy? the body will
become the enemy? Not long now not
far now. All we need to do is wait. Not
long now not far now. All we need to do
is live. All we need to do is breathe
Wait. Live. Breathe. That is all we need to do
Blow, puff, inhale, exhale, suck in air, breathe
One could say that point is birth or mid life
Or in very very very old age
When we ask a mother or a midwife
Or someone who is at that ending stage
They would agree: the breaking point lays ahead
Or maybe that point comes when you're long dead

The Post

I am of that very generation
That saw arrive by post an envelope
containing life, death, love, invitations
celebrations, potential and hope...
The thin blue paper of an airmail one
Brought news from the other side of the globe
The thick, stiff, heavy, half open white ones
smelled of soap and brought a kaleidoscope
of exciting possible notes about
weddings and birthday parties and births
Such messages travelled quite a route
From all corners of the country and earth
Licking the stamp and the envelope's tail
I would dream of the one who'd receive mail

We Are Asymmetrical

At my centre I am completely still
To you it seems that I turn but to me
It is the whole world that around me mills
We are asymmetrical, you and me
When I walk you see me move but to me
The pavement moves. I move a big spheroid
around under my walking feet, you see?
It's moved by me, a mover on steroids
To you, the train moves to my destination
To me, my destination moves to me
To you, a train clearly leaves the station
But the station leaves the train for me
We are not really face to face, you see
Instead, we are face to space, you and me

My Mother and Red Current

How my mother loves red currant berries
She shrieks in the store when they have arrived
How her mood instantly becomes merry
She claps her hands in surprise and describes
The dessert she is going to prepare
Vanilla custard, cream and red currant
In the kitchen she takes infinite care
Constantly praising the pure red fragrance
In little glass bowls she pours the custard
Forms a white patch of cream in the middle
Places the berries with cheeks as flustered
as the berries. So red. She fiddles
Until the wee bowls look like works of art
They are served with a piece of butter tart

Singing

Singing is better than sex. When done well
It sets my entire body on fire
And all my skin, every single cell
When I am harmonising in a choir
It doesn't take much. Everyone can sing
Harmonising takes a tiny bit more
I just do my best and there comes the sting
in my heart that ignites and burns my core
The sensation feels like strong vertigo
A high-pitched metal grip around my chest
That spreads downwards as the music flows
As if I'm standing on a rooftop's edge
Here come the shivers, tears, quivers and joy
that rush from my centre to my skin
when I perceive the harmony, oh boy!
Quite against my will, I begin to grin
It's like an explosion in slow motion
a tremendous, powerful emotion

A Three Dog Day

Today is a day fit for closing my eyes
Leave the computer alone, my thesis
folder shut. Replenish mental supplies
A day that flows by without any fizz
A day like a river on a hot day
A day like a desert on a cold night
A day like a long-deserted highway
A three-dog day without strive, bite or fight
A day to dwell on my dreams of last night
A day to linger and order food in
A day to not think and dim any light
A day like a mountain lake, the origin
of suspended downhill streams that begin
running when I return to discipline

Ex

You were like an ill-fitting pair of shoes
Only remembered for their discomfort
You were rather good looking like these shoes
And like these shoes, did not do an effort
Extremely unaccommodating you
drove me down and soon to gloomy despair
Like these shoes, you made me feel sad and blue
And like that shit pair, you made me not care
You were hard, tough, stiff and unbending
Rigid and unyielding like cheap leather
Frigid, inelastic, set, pretending
To be hip and artsy and together
I could not take them off, remember?
You had to pull, peel them from my feet
To no avail, you nearly dismembered
me, tore me apart. A fiasco complete
I staggered around blind in your presence
Blistered and hankering for your absence

Retirement

In ten days, a sea of time will open
My freedom will be written by her waves
A tabloid of bobbing blue unbroken
stretches all the way forward, to the grave
We, the old, are lucky in this country
Mother Australia provides for us
through a pension, rather plenty
for the sixty-seven-year-old plus
Since I have done everything I wanted
when I was younger, my wishes are few
some seeds for what I want I have planted
for this dwelling before the new blue view
I will follow the whales on my new trails
And on Saturdays go to the lawn sales

Exactly What I Want

Within the bound'ries of a doll on a string
I do exactly what I want to do
This seems to make some people mad and sting:
'Yeah that's what we *all* want to do.' I coo:
'Yes, and I *do* what we all want to do'
'That's bloody easy', they quickly reply
'What should I then? Do what *you* want to do?'
'It is just too fucken easy,' they sigh
I say: 'Why don't you try it for a change'
They look at me as if I am insane
or at least temporarily deranged
'Don't be ridiculous', they surly state
Doing just what one wants is a taboo!
I wonder when that began to be true?

Rothko Exhibition

It rains sun rays. It hails boiling beams
The horny wind makes the dark sky pregnant
The murky night turns over while it dreams
of splitting open, birth of stars imminent...
Horizons vague like fluctuating rifts
lock like a door to a cell in prison
Just letting through a moon ray swift
not strong enough to strangle the vision
What did the brushes want with the paint, how
to break stagnant storms, better still, bend them
While white eyes listen to how the snow howls
and fingers sing a country-less anthem
Where do these simmering square-ish fields lead
but to another? Paths of scents that bleed
colour into one another.....

Puppets

I knew for while that we're all puppets
Animals, humans, plants, fungi, and trees
Puppets on strings, or hand-steered like muppets
None of us is ultimately free
Strings are epigenetic; genetic
We are entirely controlled by them
Whether we are athletic, poetic
depends on our genes and social system
It makes us magnetic or pathetic
energetic, lazy, clever, or dumb
Any change is merely cosmetic
What counts is the villa-street or the slum
I didn't expect that the more I sing
I don't see puppets but rather the strings

How Adults Talk to Babies

Ah boe boe boe boe Ah boe boe boe boe
Wa dja dja dja dja Wa dja dja dja dja
Cohoo, yeah, cohoo, cohoo, yeah cohoo
Hmwa ma ma ma ma hmmwa ma ma ma
Eh yeahhhh, eh yeahhhh, eh yeahhhhh, eh yeahhhh, eh yeahhhh
Dada dada dada dada dada dada
Pooo pooo? Yeah? Poo pooo? Yeah? Pooo poooh? Yeah?
Kakakaka koooo papa, kakakaka koooo papa
Osh osh osh cuuuuuutipie osh cuuuutipie
I luuuuuuve yu! I luuuuuve yu! Yeah! I luuuuuuve yu!
Yeah, flap flap flap fly fly fly fly fly
Booh booh booh booh booh bo boooooooh!
Kika kika kika kika kika booooooh

Simpson Desert

In my swag I watch how the stars travel
along the night sky, not caring at all
whether we live, thrive, die, or unravel
a passing morning cloud makes me feel small
it continues on its way, not giving
a flying fuck about what lays below
the almost dead, the dead, and the living
until an uncaring pregnant wind blows
it away and scatters it across the sky
looking down on us like one big blue eye
watching our suffering, uncaring and dry
while a haughty and arrogant sun fries
my hat, while I step on tiny beings
who have towards me similar feelings

Phoning Faye

Phoning Faye usually takes two hours
or more. First, we establish what is new
Then we discuss who died, friends of ours
Then we establish some general truths
Like who/what has the right to existence
Art: good if it is good, 'woke' is a 'no'
We state our acceptance & resistance
We have fun, we laugh, we are in the flow
But then somehow, at some point, we always
begin dragging up old friends, now frenemies
and end up in a vague daze, a mind haze
and dig up old dead stinking memories
We have learned that there the phone call must end
Or else we send ourselves around the bend

Old Male Friends

Some old male friends feel compelled to tell jokes
When having a chat with a female friend
In me this compulsive joking provokes
Nausea; anxiety; it offends
I find it as stupid as mansplaining
Especially when the jokes are pompous
I feel I must quickly start explaining
why the obsession is so obnoxious
Why do these clowns need to entertain us?
Why do we have to titter with their jokes?
They do it for *them* and not for us
I feel like saying: please, please stop it folks
I cannot force myself to laugh, you see
For heaven's sake, please, please, let me be!

Short-Circuited

On my way to see my lover I met
a young boy I instantly fell in love with
I turned my stone into a heart, was set
to love them both. I said to the kid:
'What about a coffee in a cafe?'
'Alas', he said, 'I am on my way
to a date that I cannot quite cancel'
'I text you a bit later then, maybe?'
With his number in my phone, I took off
etched in my brain and heart was this baby
I continued my way to my Beau
where I met the boy again… there was a row

Aristotle's Riddle

Think about time as divided into
the future, the present and the past
the past does not exist, this is true
how thick is the 'now', how long does it last?
The future does not exist, this is true
So, the present is something or a no-thing
in an endless nothing, not old, not new
So, time seems to be a nothing and a nothing
Connected by a no-thing, how can that be?
The now is the outer edge of the past
That does not exist. It also is, gee!
The nearest edge of the future, blast!
That does not exist, this means that the 'now'
Does not at all exist either, wow, wow!

How God Travelled

First God lived in the rocks, the plants, the trees
Her whispered wishes could clearly be heard
Her commands were carried on by a breeze
By water or on the wings of a bird
God was in kitchen, toilet and attic
was fed rice, fresh shoots, sake, and peaches
She stayed in these places sure and static
The object of speeches by lay preachers
Then she gradually moved toward the sky
To the distant blue just beyond the clouds
A hovering eye or simply a lie
Some kept believing while others had doubts
Now, She dwells at the edges of space/time
She may move any moment in time again

The Lime Tree

Our neighbour hates leaves on his concrete slabs
A blower in each hand, he keeps them clean
With a chainsaw over the fence, he back stabs
our lime tree, and we can't intervene
The tree is full of cute little limes
When the bastard cowardice attacks it
An embittered, hostile, acerbic crime
He nearly halves the rich, lush canopy
After the unspeakable deed, he stacks
screaming branches on the back of his Ute
while we, still paralysed by the attack
stand in the street, observing how the brute
leaves a trail of yellow and green jewels
we wave the tangled limbs, stems, and twigs farewell

The Ghan Departs

The desert is cut by the endless train
Under an inpatient sky full of clouds
God knows we desperately need rain
The swollen Todd will need the happy crowds
The parched desert is vast, fast asleep
Its' dusty breath creeps swift up the windows
Lightning clatters, thunder screams, the rain weeps
Watery arrows gather in hollows
I open the window, water fragrance
mixed with dust, only here, yes, only here
Red radiance, on the roof a cadence
Red brilliance, as rain on windows tears
I watch how the desert pours into me
Until Adelaide washes over me

She is Something Else

Her love for me is unconditional
She always has my back, no matter what
She is so vastly nutritional
She is a love and nurture acrobat
She is so exceptionally loyal
There's no shilly-shally in her support
She is a caring Comrade Royale
There is no end to her gentle effort
There's no softness or weakness in her love
Steady as a tree, supple as bamboo
Persistently and when push comes to shove
she sees every situation trough
It is easy to love her, the beloved
Extraordinary to be so loved

Retired!

Today I retired from my day job
Before me lies a vast stretch of space/time
In which I am going to jump and bob
while lying on my back and rhyme
Well, I still have my own firm to tend to
Oh, and my PhD thesis to write
But the absence of pressure is new
I feel unusually relieved and light
No obstacles any longer before
what I truly wish to engage with
No more laborious chores to slough through
And not unimportant: time to breathe
Sure, it should be like this all our lives long
With the world of work is something quite wrong

Quick, Call the Priest!

When you look at Nixon or George W Bush
And think they were not too bad, is a sign
of our time, now that Trump attempts a push
for the white house again. They seem benign
in comparison to what we see now
The blatant, shameless absence of good taste
and decency we arrived at somehow
after America was briefly graced
with Michelle and Barak Obama
What a great gulp of fresh air that was
Mama, spare us the upcoming drama
of the orange orangutan, my ass
Imagine him stirring in the Middle East
Or Ukraine-Russia. Quick, call the priest!

Love is Blind

It is late afternoon; I feel like some
very bad TV. My sons and I once
developed the habit of watching some
crap TV, mainly dubious romance
My fave bad TV show *Love is Blind*
may have dropped on Netflix, so if else fails...
I will submerge myself in the kind
of emotions of those that wear fake nails
Botox faces, balloon lips, silicon bits
I will emerge refreshed from the glitter
gowns, heels, tattoos and half exposed tits
Sit it out, persevere, not a quitter
And after my thirst for kitsch is quenched
In learned papers I will be drenched

When Feeling Triggered

In case of tension, instead of triggers
(To be 'triggered' is so eh triggering)
Look for sparks and look for glimmers
(To feel triggered is so off-putting)
Where there's darkness there is also light
Sometimes only little pinpoints, that's true
But small lights are like diamonds bright
Like stars in the night, that guide you through
Glimmers are the opposite of triggers
small moments that spark opposite emotions
joy, peace and safety that may cause jiggers
and open up rivers of flow, oceans
Try it next time you feel triggered and blue
I guarantee you, you will feel anew

Thing-Flings

Another evil of the sixties and
seventies is growing consumerism
Even music became something to be consumed
Emotions arise with consumerism
Firstly, there is the anticipation
Then the inevitable dopamine hit
of having the wanted in possession
This doesn't last long, you better believe it
A dive to indifference and dislike
unescapably follows. The desired thing
is ditched to make room for the next spike
Some people can't do the ditching
They are called 'hoarders,' prisoners of things
Ultimate slavery; burned wings, puppet-strings
Velcro-clings, thing-flings…

The Dance the Body Remembers

Every night, in its mind, it dances
It paints itself white with flour paste
It blackens the inside of its mouth, dense
its lips are thin and brightly glazed
It wears a ripped white dress with red lining
It releases itself to the elements
Bare footed, it begins designing, shining
and communing with its environment
It takes no shape or form directed by
the mind or art. It finds its own way
It reaches to the sky, as if to defy
the earth, the soil, the dirt, the sand, the clay
Then folds against the wind, a hurricane
arms float everywhere, hair raising, waiving
hands, dripping, beaten down by heavy rain
Feet painting an irregular craving
Flexibly following weather tempers
It dances the dance the body remembers

Dance with the Cold

Body enters a forest of crisscross
bamboo. Leaves whisper, stalks dully clatter
Feet tiptoe light on a carpet of moss
Arms moved by wind, hands follow, fingers flow
Knees shake, hair streams, limbs shivers with cold
Body surrenders, still as a curved stone
at first, then moves forwards, contracts, shrinks, rolls
in slow motion, alone, just flesh on bone
Not driven by mind, soul, spirit or self
but by complex forces outside itself
it simply finds its own way by itself
shedding its ego, light now as an elf
With the psyche discarded, still and serene
the movements now show the space in between

Dancing the Red Line

The body, it steps onto the red line
Arms have a life of their own for balance
On one foot a high heeled shoe which aligns
The other black bare foot counterbalances
The line is on fire, disintegrates
into the void beneath it, it hangs on
by its spine, almost obliterated
almost dead, almost silenced, almost gone
The eyes in the white face cross to the max
the blackened mouth gasps wide and wild
the burning fingers seem hanging relaxed
The skin slowly melts, drips, pink piles
A child silently stands by the boiling liquid
Hiroshima Mon Amour revisited

Performance in Brussels 1983

Two naked bodies are born from the hatch
in the ceiling. Legs first. They drop slowly
A boy? A girl? Wait! They wear tops, they match
Hoodies. Red scarves? Slowly, they plunge lower
Someone in the audience screams. The two
crash to the stage 'bout two meters below
Roll around like river stones. Who is who?
They do not dance, really, but rather flow
Antennas, bald, smooth, rock-like and seeking
Like walkie talkies they find each other
Wind and water seem to rock them gently
Sister and brother? Infant and mother?
The dance seems to exist in between them
They seem part of a body weather system

Gravity

I am weightless in my dreams, effortless
I move through spaces, flying, flowing
My hands and feet are errorless
While I am going; speeding and slowing
Thinking and talking are one and the same
Tasting, feeling, hearing and smelling too
I have neither form nor shape, frame, bones, name
I fit through every narrow alley, I pursue
(dissociated from my waking self)
communication with other such elves
Who equally don't have a soul or a self
Then I wake up and return to 'myself'
Which is heavy with bones, thoughts and 'myself'
Who is the real one? I often ask myself

Rabbit Hole

Woke up with a start, full of good insights
for my thesis. As usual I had to immediately
quickly, speedily, dot down the highlights
then fill in the gaps obediently
From one little thought came another one
Then ten, then hundred. I call this 'a bloom'
Branches grew and became part of the plan
It was not a bloom, it was rather a boom
Down down down the rabbit hole I wandered
Until my stomach began to yodel
When twelve-hundred concepts I had pondered
I had to put down my new-found model
It was four in the morning when I began
It's pitch dark now, you better eat, Suzanne

At Home in the World

Do you feel at home in this world? I
was asked. If with 'at home' is meant 'at ease'
I would answer 'no'. But how then do I
feel really? Do I feel it's all a breeze?
No. I seem to only be able to find
notions which instil the answer 'no' but
to which notion would I say 'yes' blind
What do you mean by 'the world' but?
If 'the world' means 'my town', then I say: 'yes'
If 'the world' means 'my skin', then I say: 'no'
If 'the world' means 'my house', then I say: 'yes'
If 'the world' means 'my land', then I say: 'no'
The strange thing is, you see, I am not in the world
But the world is in me. I don't own the land
But it owns me

Bob

The best boss I ever had was boss Bob
Husband of Dee, father of twins, boss of me
Because of Bob I loved my job, and Bob
A Baptist minister from Kansas was he
His smiling face was round and kind and nice
His eyes twinkled with mischief and mirth
His language was humorous and precise
His voice was loud and clear and full of wit
He died eight years ago, I read today
Dee seems still around and so are the twins
What a loss. And what a great lot were they
His three beloved girls now without their prince
Bob, you were the best! You wonderful man
Send a postcard from heaven if you can

Today

The day began pouting, like a man who
didn't get his way. A tear escaped his eye
but gradually the sullen mood gave way to
a multitude of rays, the sun's bright light
spread like a sheet laid over town and land
Thus began this day. People, on their way
followed the trails of the stars in the sand
to work or play or pay or obey
Like when a curtain slides open, the old story
as new revealed itself. In all its glory

You and Me

From a first-person view and perspective
I can see clearly that I have no head
Try it, you must be very objective
You look out of a no-head instead
We are taught to use the third-person view
To view ourselves, this, however, is untrue
The other should be the object of this view
The other has a head, yes, this is true
There is space instead of a head, for me
But you have a head, that is, for me
For you, there is space where your head must be
That's why we are different, you and me
Seeing a head where there is none, makes you
feel like you are a *thing*; this makes you blue

What Rests

Her eyes close slowly, deep in the last light
she sees eternity, drowns in mirages
of her long path and its side tracks, the sights
the last word has been said. The last visages
What remains is the panting of the chest
that belatedly falls silent, the doctor
feels the pulse, notes the hour, lets her rest
She is no longer an actor or conductor
Slowly, she changes from a person
into a stone. Improved or worsened?

In Spirit

We departed after the bubble burst
As Chris said, in spirit, we never left
Internally, we remained deeply immersed
Externally, we feel forever bereft
We go on plunging, dunking, submerging
ourselves in language, custom, form
splurging, resurging, indulging, immerging
A warm storm that continues to transform
Nothing left on us all a clearer mark
Like a fire mark burned in youthful flesh
We embarked on something sparkling dark
We experience it over again, fresh
Japan, we could not have left you, even
if we tried. To you, forever driven

Indian Winter

Why, oh by God, this Indian Winter?
This dip in temperature when all
doonas are stored and all socks are hinter
and heaters are uninstalled from the wall
And jumpers are in bags with lavender
And old leggings are thrown in the trash
And the absence of woollens engenders
a stashing of towels of which the backlash
is that if they are slightly wet, they are freezing
so one is forced to use the oven heat
for squeezing the water out and teasing
while my feet are freezing under my sheet
Bring on the ardour from the sun, I say
Better sooner than later, yes, okay?

One Bitter Line

Fuck lass, you just poured ice over the sun
Shit miss, you made the bee loose its sting
You managed to, in one line, kill the fun
You stole from the music all its swing
You dried the rain with your angry breath
Melted the ice with your discontent
Caused the stars to fall to their death
You turned the river into cement
the bed into fire, the milk into vinegar
my warm flesh into ash and stone
You ripped into my skin a nasty scar
Just because I wasn't coming to the phone
You flatten mountains to get it your way
And that, mademoiselle, is not okay

The Key of Me

The day hesitates, some rain in between
A sun that is hiding behind clouds
The blue of the sky is pale, it seems
Winter is on its last legs, the clouds sound
like violin strings on the veins of leaves
The day weighs like lead, inland the mind moves
thin is the imagination, thieves
stole the desire of the sun to improve
The cyclist at the stop sign hesitates
The river sand turns red into grey
Even the trees seem to hesitate
Play seems to stagnate, visitors stay
The night tries to decide what to be
Midnight tries to find the key of me

Merci

Thank you, seashells for being so pretty
Grazie, all dogs for walking by my side
Dank je, Tokyo for being an awesome city
Gamsahamnida, horses for wild and brilliant rides
To sweet juicy fat blackberries, merci
Mustard coloured butter-soft ankle boots
Danke! Gracias, sea for the swims in Thee
Arigatou, beautiful bowls with fruits
Obrigado, fresh flowers in vases
Спасибо for the thrill of singing songs
For the faces of babies I say: Dhonnobad
For the courage of the old I say: شكراً
Kia ora, animals just for being
תודה eyes for all that seeing

What is Real?

When evening comes and heavily falls
over me. The night air stretches lazily
there is a dream waiting for me, it rolls
towards me; a pearl in an oyster shell
I close the gates of my head and lay down
carefully in the soft flesh of the dream
pulling my gown tied around me, I frown
at the clown that visits me. A loud scream
almost wakes me from my elastic bed
but I realise, in lucid dream, that
I am only dreaming and the fat bat
that is flying into my hair is just that
A dream. Or is this the reality?
Is waking a dream, in all its brutality?

Arigatou!

To books, big and smaller, I say: Thank you!
Dank U! I say to all birds for singing
Tak! For sitting there being the pretty coo
To Talking Heads, Merci! for your swinging
Gamsahamnida! Deep river that held us
bobbing on tyres and chatting to dabbled
sunlight till we shivered, so much to discuss
Dhanyavaad! game of Scrabble
Featherdown doonas, Teşekkür ederim!
Dziękuję! splinters of sound and singing
on a Sunday, a fragment of a hymn
Xièxiè! Amsterdam and the tower bell ringing
Henry Purcell, spasibo! For the unheard
beauty. And thank you God for the WORD

Köszönöm!

Starry nights in the desert, Köszönöm!
Fresh fruit juices, Merci! You rock it
Ευχαριστώ, Larry Anderson in concert
Takk, smooth round river rock in my pocket
Хвала, Barak Obama and Michelle
Kia ora, kittens and puppy swarms
Go raibh maith agat, Sebastian and Belle
Khop khun, sustainable justice reforms
Shukran, Alice Springs, you are the best
Mulțumesc, gum trees and your scent
Děkuji, little naked birds in nests
Terima kasih, new laws of consent
Bamboo pens, bistre and washi, Хвала!
Japanese wrapping furoshiki, Dankon!

The Cold Press Juicer

Mandarin, pear and watermelon
Mamamia, what an exquisite blend
And that was only the beginning. Lemon,
mint, nashi and pineapple were next
I could play all day with this novel toy
It makes fresh pasta too and nut butter
It turns any fruit into ice-cream to enjoy
I am def an instant cold press nutter
It prepares bread dough, and it minces
The motor rotates like a Toyota
Unsure, at first it took some convincing
I bought top of the range, hooray
I know: Quality always pays off
But sometimes I forget that and then I scoff

Chez Nous

Croissants, baguette, beurre de Barette
La Vache qui rit, Chat Noir, Côte d'Or
Stassano, Chiquita, omelette
Speculaas, Pâté en Croûte
La Libre Belgique, Femmes d'Aujourd'hui
Talking Heads, Georges Brassens, Miles....
Tintin, Charles Trenet, Croissant farci
Our best clothes in ska and punk styles
Le déjeuner a l'ombre de monsieur et madame
Van Severen – Visser et leurs enfants
des années 70 aux années 60, ham & jam
du siècle dernier; more croissants
We were poor wee artists but on Sundays:
Mousses, soufflés, purées, parfaits, sundaes....

After a poem by Guido Lauwaert, that bastard

Me

I realise that I have quite become
the main subject of all my writing
Less interested in fiction I've become
Myself, however, I find exciting
Although my mind is like an empty room
in a large and crumbling old mansion
The wind that blows through it knows no gloom
through shattered windows, it's full of action
Images, words, sounds, smells and memories
On the flow of wind through that space roam
Forming poems, stories and allegories
Fiction is a thing of hope; hope for change
for a thrill, to produce Art, to me that's strange....

Japanese Potato Salad

Wow, that Japanese potato salad
I made today, was almost perfect
So satisfying it deserves a ballad
The lukewarm fluffiness has that effect
Freshly pickled cucumber for freshness
Little soft cubes of carrot for colour
Course black pepper for greatness and wholeness
Popping yellow corn for a hint of sweetness
The potatoes not mushy but chunky
Boiled eggs for extra creaminess, richness
Some green beans to make it more funky
This combination heals any illness
Served almost warm with kewpie and mustard
I emerged from eating it quite lustred

Coffee with a Layer of Cream

Thank you, coffee with a layer of cream
Merci, warm sun on the back of my dress
Danke, colourful, adventurous dream
Diolch, every little piece of success
Cats of this world, go raibh maith agat
Carles Ives symphonies, domo arigatou
Great universities, salamat
Ink on washi, Dank U!
Malayalam, little girls in pretty dresses
Mulțumesc, smiling face in the street
Хвала, mushrooms for treating stresses
Takk, things that are complete
Gamsahamnida! volcanoes
Terima kasih, Steinway grand pianos

Like Bread So Sweet

As we are kneaded by the hands of age
Turned, slapped, spread, rolled, abandoned, returned to
We become kinder; lose most of our rage
Instead of wanting love, like, we yearn to
Live in accord with ourselves and others
While we are stomped, pinched, proved and heated
We long for sisters and for brothers
While the hands of time relentlessly repeat
the pressing, rubbing, squeezing, massaging
We temper, soften, relax, and melt
When the pressure is quite unrelenting
We prepare to embrace, hold and be held
When we are finally baked, we are sweet
saints almost, our voyage nearly complete

Suddenly

It is Sunday. The weather is quite dark
We may be getting rain. The street is quite
quiet. The birds too. Nothing holds a spark
The chooks are laying low too, like at night
The daily chores are done, I'm winding down
A pasta bake is in the fridge for three
four days at least, the house is clean, the town
seems frozen in time, nothing to see
I drum a rhythm with my fingers
on the titanium of my Apple Mac
greyish light seeps in and lingers
It is a day to be limp and slack
I search the ceiling for some sort of sign
The sun breaks in, the birds wake up: sublime!

Morning Routine

Retirement means that morning routines
can be so pleasurable and endless
silent and alone, so nobody screens
a particular kind of morning bliss
I linger in bed and write a sonnet
update the Alice Springs Bulletin Board
try to find a rhyme word for "sonnet"
in The Conversation, I read WAR, Lord!
I read some of my thesis with intention
to edit, check my mail, still excusing
Then my body wants s u d d e n attention
Movement. I begin the daily juicing
Celery, beetroot, apple and ginger
And can't find a word that rhymes with "ginger"

Millions of Little Universes

Tokyo consists of millions of little
universes, each with their own unique
atmosphere. Some robust, others brittle
Tiny coffee shops with their own mystique
Small bars, miniature cafes, petite
taverns, pocket-sized snack bars, most of them
specialised in one thing only: sex, fluffy sweets
drip-through coffee with vanilla slice, reggae
whisky, or *matcha* with soybean chews
Pussy Cat is one of these universes
Specialised in a Japanese version of Blues
It swallows you when you enter it, curses
you, when you go down the narrow stairs that
leads from always buzzing Tamachi Dori
you are eaten alive; by Pussy Cat
spat into a small *kenkan*, there begins the story
behind a heavy wooden door with copper
fixtures all over it. Along the way down
noise from the street dims, the bar hopper
comes to a complete halt, the town vanishes
the staircase bends; a brief no-man's-land
only a few seconds of silence
The kitsch door opens the sound of a band
A choir of voices. A framed licence
Calling out: "*Irrashaimasen*" Welcome!
Hostesses fuss. The evening blossoms...

My Mum's Chicory Salad

The sharp bitterness of raw chicory
The tartness of apples and their sweetness
Start off this super-salad story
We strive for perfection and completeness
Dice in some cold boiled beetroot for redness
Some hard-boiled eggs for creaminess
Kewpi mayo for super-salad madness
A few drops of mustard for extra sharpness
You could add walnuts if you wanted to
Or little blocks of extra bity cheese
Some curry powder or old Stilton Blue
But do this only if you so please
Add salt and white pepper to perfect it
Let it sit a bit then start eating it

Poor Mailboxes

Mailboxes once were like kitchen tables
A lively central point of the household
A place where yarns, stories and fables
came together and were told and retold
Now mailboxes only receive rubbish
The occasional old-fashioned flyer
In which we wrap our rotten veg & fish
Once the domain of the town criers
They wither derelict and abandoned
At entrances of gardens & properties
Like wilted flowers, they look stranded
Forgotten and ignored anomalies
There is an entire generation
Who never felt the rousing sensation
of getting a letter

Peeling Broad Beans

Yay! They are for sale at Produce Pete
Huge fresh broad beans in their leggy peels
Today, I raced down to Produce Pete's street
I'd almost forgotten how those peels feel
The fresh snap when I strangled them softly
The ropy veins by which I opened them
The insides of the peels, silky and soft
The beans rest inside like a row of gems
In green canoes lined with white velvet
I touched the kidney-shaped treasures ever so gently
Lifting them from their moist silken beds
I stirred them awake with a soft caress
Anticipating their deep bittersweetness
I added a little sage for completeness

Second Childhood

I have fun now. I am enjoying my
second childhood. I am just learning to
play again, to be happy, merry, high
and only doing what I want to do
Looking. Seeing. Being in the body
being alive, not being afraid, free...
learned to be alone and need nobody
behind me a war, before me the sea
There's a stigma on being alone
I simply don't give a fuck. Stigmatise
as much as you want. This rolling stone
it won't touch. I invent and improvise
Drunk by a lack of stress, blindfolded
I explore what night holds, day unfolds

Things That Make You Rich

A whiff of fresh wind after a hot day
The swelling, deep breathing of the sea
The cute way in which kittens play
The things that make you rich are wholly free
The touch of a jumper after a chill
After hours of seeking finding the key
When being hungry taking your fill
The things that make you rich are fully free
The desert during a wildflower burst
That your ears can hear, your eyes can see
The first gulps of a drink after thirst
The things that make you rich are utterly free
Climbing slowly to the top of a tree
Things that make you rich are completely free

The Not-Seen

We need the eyes of others to see what
is in front of us. My boring street can be
a marvel for another. Your son-brat
an adorable Adonis to me
Sometime a stranger takes you to a place
in a city where you have lived for years
that you've never been, a place of such grace
and splendour that it brings you to tears
I remember the first time I tasted
Shiso in Japan. It was most magic
While many treated it as deco waste
This vicarious looking can be tragic
It is why travel is so seductive
The unfamiliar is attractive

Unknowable

I am unknowable even to myself
A walking riddle, a sack made of skin
We are unknowable even to ourselves
Filled with stuff and blood to the very rim
There is absolutely no room left for
A soul or a spirit or a self
So stuffed are we with stuff, therefor
When asked who I am, what should I say?
I can say my name, but what does that mean?
We can tell you our age, but what does that mean?
I can say where I live, but what does that mean?
We can take a selfie, but what does that show?
At our centre we are empty, stuff
shows up in that emptiness, stuff, stuff, stuff

Whatever My Eye Can See

Whatever my eye can see, is mine
at least for a while. Eye own everything
eye see. That high mountain is mine
That vast sea is mine, really anything
eye see, eye own for a second or three
that gigantic rock over there, you see?
That majestic tree in the lee, all belong to me
Eye only have to be and see to see
The aquamarine sky is wholly mine
The stars, the sun and the moon eye can see
they are, by their very design, mine
in all their shiny and shimmering glee
Eye do not need much else or more or less
Eye just need these things to soar and adore

To Seek Refuge by Thyself

Most traffic in the streets is there because
of the fear of man of being alone; man seeks
company, friendship, love, follows the laws
of loneliness, he travels for weeks
to escape himself and meet the other
Why not seek refuge by thyself, I say
Why cozy up, rub shoulders, smother
the other? Why not fearlessly stay
with thyself and let the grass grow between
the stones of the streets where traffic races
from one dwelling to another. Let green
shoot up in the cracks, avoid embraces
Let silence encroach on the streets while thy
cry, die of loneliness, sigh, ah tell me why

The Scorn of Yuletide

What mockery doth Yuletide joy reveal
    With baubles bright and hollow carols sung?
A gilded mask on commerce's cold appeal
Where greed o'ershadows hearts where love hath clung
The crowded streets with weary souls oppressed
In frenzied chase of trinkets wrapped in lies
No solace found, no moment's quiet rest
'Tis but a feast where shallow pleasures rise
The winter's chill, though fair, feels false and grim
Beneath the tinsel's glow, a world decayed
The jolly mirth, a thin and fleeting hymn
A fleeting spark that leaves the soul betrayed
Yet lo, my hate for Christmas doth disguise
A longing for its truth, unspoiled, to rise

Anti-natalism

Anti-natalists see procreation
As an act of savage violence
A consentless and dumb celebration
A disturbance of a peaceful absence
Bring a child into this harsh, cruel world
And it is sure and certain to suffer
It arrives with its body wholly curled
As if it knows it will get tougher, rougher
The amount of suffering in a life
Far outnumbers happy, blissful moments
While in the before-life and after-life
There cannot be suffering or enjoyment
It is better not to be born at all
Procreation: men's ultimate downfall

Old Men and Books

Male friends my age often like paper books
They have hundreds or even thousands
Cookbooks, storybooks, scrapbooks, textbooks
Guidebooks, art books, novels that no human hands
have touched in years. They are the cat-ladies
amongst old men. Their places reek of paper
slowly eaten by mites and silverfish
usually stacks of yellowed newspapers
live alongside their volumes and tomes
manuscripts, hardcovers and paperbacks
have taken over their entire homes
Shelves and racks full of stacks and packs
They are proud that they physically own
Tons of paper that'd fit in their phone

Not Long Anymore

Our thoughts are still free. Who would guess them?
They dance by like nightly shadows. No man
can touch them, no hunter can shoot them
No one can trace them, nobody can
We think what we want in furtive dreams
Thoughts' sweetness flows quietly through our blood
Our wishes and desires softly stream
Let them be an endless gentle flood
Enthrals us in our dark tower, worries
and trouble lost. Thoughts like fires
cause walls to crumble, mice to scurry
the roof to cave in, in thoughts our desire
For them and us and she and he and thee
One thing is certain: our thoughts are still free

After an old Dutch song
De gedachten zijn vrij

Modern Medicine

I went to see the doctor for back pain
I hadn't been for sixteen years or so
I'm not quite sure what I hoped to gain
I first wanted to exclude some things so
After telling doc my pain history
I let doc first throw some things at me
For doc it was not much of a mystery
For me to have a shot at being pain free
I must collect my poo 3x to rule out
bowel cancer. I must collect my midstream pee
for pee pee tracks and bladder to be ruled out
And they will test my blood too, you see
They will look at my bone density
My female organs will be scrutinised
And while at it, they will examine my kidneys
Then an MRI scan will be organised
While checking my collected poop
they will scan my never scanned boobs
And several random veins and tubes
And get out the gloves and the lube
Leaving doc's office with forms galore
I had quite forgotten what I had come in for

Stuff

Why do people hoard so much stuff, I ask
A false sense of security, I say
They use their house full of stuff as a mask
They can't keep their accumulating at bay
It is a serious issue: cluttered minds
Cluttered homes and, ultimately: Cluttered
Earth. They are urgently reminded
That "away" as in "throw away", I uttered
Is not a no-place. "Away" is a place
Where clutter goes after it is thrown away
The resulting mess an utter disgrace
Stop buying all that stuff, make my day
People, get your fucking act together
Or we will together perish in extreme weather

Freedom

A house full of stuff and a top-notch car
Are the status symbols of the near past
Now, people begin to realise that
Freedom is the thing that may better last
Freedom of choice, freedom of time, of place
Do what you want, when you want, where you want
Quit the house-stuff-car eternal rat race
Quite the shit-myth of grow-expand-demand
Freedom of stuff, things, shit, junk, gear, and kit
Freedom of equipment, objects, tackle
Freedom of pack, cram, ram, jam, and stow shit
Freedom of property, throw off that shackle
Possessions, belongings: out of fashion!
Freedom, time, space, to pursue your passion

Tooth Elf

Peta is the tooth fairy in our town
She makes a gloomy smile shine bright again
Don't frown when your teeth are green or brown
Peta has you covered without pain
If truth be told, she is a sculptor
She shapes live-like gums and great looking teeth
She is the nearly poetic author
Of a mouthful of excellent teeth
All her utensils and tools are minute
They fit on petite tiny little shelves
You will leave the place in good tooth spirits
Let's not call her 'tooth fairy' but 'tooth elf'
You leave her practice in a better tooth mood
and in dear search for chewable food

Reminder

Don't leave anything for later. Later
the coffee is cold. Later the day turns
into night. Later, I am old. Later
Later, this moment never returns
Later, this fleeting dance is over
Regret is a bitter pill to swallow
Missed chances, unspoken words, leftovers
Let me not leave anything to follow
up on. Cherish the moments as they come
because later, the vegetables go limp
while I followed the "here comes later" drum
when to the next thing I eagerly jump
Later is a place that doesn't exist
There is real reason to resist it

Today

Today is the day. It's here only now
Tomorrow it is not today anymore
Don't complain. Enjoy, relish, allow
It's granted. We must feel this to the core
Do it today because today is *the* day
Yesterday is too late. Tomorrow too
early. Make sure to amuse, have fun, and play
What we do today is genuine and true
Yesterday may well turn into a lie
Tomorrow may well be a chaotic mess
Let's not reject, stand in the way, deny
today, because it's all we can access
Today is like a diamond so bright
All else belongs to the blackness of night

Marianne

Marianne, you don't know what you mean
to me. You are my muse, my friend, my champ
In our long slow story, you are the queen
The empress, a light from the brightest lamp
which lights our paths through the wonderlands
Of Tokyo, Amsterdam, Basel
Australia and Vienna. By your hands
An epic meeting of friends happened
A once in a lifetime event it was
In the finest bookstore of Amsterdam
Besotted, I wished then it would never pass
Pity we had no Facebook or Instagram
I've never seen photos of that event
I carry it with me in the present

Barack Obama

How did we ever dare to complain when
Barack Obama was holding the helm
Waters were calm. It was smooth sailing then
His wings were quite clipped in every realm
Still, he and Michelle radiated
A sense of calm and natural dignity
They created, stated, debated
translated so animatedly
their views, that we felt fascinated
And revelled in an era void of
scandals, it was all so elevated
compared to the current void of love
Wow, I say, how could we even allow
the downward spiral to the terror of now

The Cottage

The trees around it weave its dabbled light
Fallen leaves, birds and chooks its gentle sounds
Deafening silence surrounds it at night
As it stands at the back end of the grounds
The path towards it gently meanders
At its entrance stands a mandarin three
Of which one can pick when one wanders
off to see the bees and chooks roam free
The orange setting sun is reflected
In the windowpane of the door at dusk
It even has very fast internet
Thanks to Starlink's crazy Elon Musk
It's the very best place to reside
To live, to create, to hide inside

Japanese Poetry

Japanese poetry is different
It is the visual experience
That makes it so very magnificent
and brimming with effervescence
Besides the usual sound-based rhyme
There is the beauty of each character
A dance of black and white that is sublime
Turns a reader into a spectator
Boldly, courageously handwritten
The *kanji* prance, skip, jump, hop, and frolic
Leaving the reader/watcher quite smitten
Elated, high, thrilled or melancholic
Being both visual *and* rhyme
A Japanese poem stands still the time

Election Angst

Is the Orange Ape going to pollute
our screens again? Was one time not enough?
Will the women-hating brute-dude uproot
our minds again? Will the lying, the bluff
Begin again? I ban any image
of him from my media and socials
To limit the harm, the hurt, the damage
Together with other Neanderthals
His name will not pass over my doorstep
His narrative I kill as it arrives
I hope for a predicable misstep
One that he will not outlive or survive
I burn a candle of courage and hope
For all out there, the American folks

Olive Pink Botanical Garden

Where the buffel grass has been cleared away
Wildflowers thrive yellow, purple, and white
Desert shrubs' blue green, trees, plants array
Causes a special fractured dappled light
Wallabies inhabit the rocky hills
Bowerbirds' bowers can be found there
The lofty blue sky boils over and spills
Small white clouds into the arid, gasping air
A single crazy tourist climbs the hills
No hat, no sleeves, short pants, she'll burn her tatts
Locals gather in the shade, dusting their clothes
under mist sprinklers, having casual chats
Protected by intricate overgrowth
Time stops racing by for a little bit
Hiding from view a world full of shit

Bed Rotting

I read that Generation Z enjoys
staying in bed for an entire day
to escape the relentless calls and noise
stressed demands and claims of a modern day
Naturally, this phenomenon has drawn
the attention of doctors and psychologists
quick to offer unsolicited advice. Yawn!
"If you're staying in bed this long," say analysts
"You might be suffering from depression
Seek help!" (aka, fill our pockets). But I'm here
to offer a different perspective; an expression
of "restorative lying", my dear
Staying in bed as long as you desire
is a safe, cheap way to regain your fire

Ichi-go Ichi

Is a Japanese phrase that means "one time
one meeting" or "one opportunity
one encounter." Every moment is sublime
In our community, unity, infinity, serenity
The idea that each moment is unique
cannot be recreated. The transient
passing, ephemeral precious mystique
of every experience, radiant
It encourages full presence and
appreciation of each interaction
as one once-in-a-lifetime event
whether it's a conversation
or an action. Rooted in Zen Buddhism
it is a reminder to embrace no ism's

Remember

Remember to support the opulent banks
And the big corporations this Christmas
Make sure big banks that rank high say thanks
And corporations experience bliss
Buy yourself mad with money you don't have
Give gifts that friends and family don't need
Receive what you don't need and be a slave
By all means: Bleed and succeed to feed greed
Help corporations bring more stuff onto
this Earth, 'cause we cannot live without it
Make sure everything you buy is brand-new
Stuff with grit that doesn't last a single bit
Make sure you throw away what you get soon
Soon, we can pollute the magnificent moon

Dark Night

Last night I experienced a pain so
debilitating that I almost wept
Christ! I was queasy from head to toe
I suffered and bore and then I slept
The shit storm continued in my dreams
Violent and dark, terrifying, terrible
A dark night of the soul it truly seems
A dark night of the body, too, unbearable
The pain lived in my spine, like a wounded
animal it twisted around and around
My Lord, I though, old age, astounded
I went to meet the pain, the playground
Of injured wolves or a wake of vultures
To face whatever was the nature of this torture

Rapture

I am a warehouse bursting with paintings
I carry a sketchbook crammed with drawings
I am a treasure trove of ink taintings
I contain a million beautiful things
I hold a hundred thick fat novels
I accommodate a trillion photographs
I embraced a lot of exotic travels
I stow several choreographs
I have space for Bizen-like ceramics
I persist in singing a thousand tunes
I roll like a pig in academics
I support a dozen or so lampoons
I am so full that I'm about to rupture
I must live a million years to capture

After the Backache

When I have suffered a bout of backache
I am so beholden that I can stroll
It's so different from heartache
I have lost and retained control
A particular type of blessedness
Walking on air, paradise, heaven
Power followed feebleness, helplessness
From a dark night of the soul to cloud eleven
I am so grateful for simply walking
That I can yell, bellow, shout out loud
Hey, look I am moving, going
I'm so delighted that I'm endowed
With legs: knees, shins, calves, ankles. Feet in shoes
Gone is the pain, vanished the blues

Mother

She is a mystery to me, a riddle
Oh, Mother, please reveal thyself to me
I know thee so intimate, thy smell
Ever so fishy, female, so She
So milky, overlaid with puff-powder
And a hint of thy honeyed perfume
Wherein lay thy force, thy power?
Something interrupted thy blossom bloom
Here, let me hold thee, like thou once held me
Here, here, we don't have to talk, just caress
Please, please hear my plea, give me the key
To thy locked chest, give me access
Give, give me that fluttering heart of thine
Put your hand in mine, pour your soul into mine
Mother, please!

Sister Drunk on the Floor

Oh, Sister, why are you so sozzled drunk
So smashed, well-oiled, tanked-up, plastered, sloshed
Oh, Sister, you became such a f-ing junk
So bombed, legless, intoxicated, washed
We can only see your loadeness, your
being stewed, sousedness, crockedness, lit
On the floor on the floor, on the floor, floor
After you've taken from a tea mug a hit
God, help my sister, because I cannot
Rock bottom has passed long ago. She sips
and gulps, slips to the floor oh floor. I cannot
but I ought to save you. But you swigged
the children away, you slurped the children
away, you gulped the children away, you glogged
the children away......and us

Sonnet With an Extra Word at the End

Teeth, today they are your friend, tomorrow
they suddenly are your worst enemy
Where they once stood crisp and half burrowed
They now dance in chaos & entropy
Time to end their lives swiftly, I ventured
To the dentist one last miserable time
Six teeth, six holes and three stitches later
I definitely hated their dumb design
First the numbing fluid then the needles
Then the pulling, the rocking, the shaking
The horrible deadly noises, needless
To say, were extremely traumatising
The throbbing pain kicked in only later
when the craters got agitated
Like volcanoes

Witlof

Grown in pitch dark, the white, soft, bitter leaves
Melt in your mouth. Once exposed to the light
They grow light green and the tightly rolled sleeves
Unfold, curl, darken and become endive leaves
Dark roots appear at the foot and thicken
The curly bouquet opens and can be
eaten too. A different bitter with
a crunch. I am a fan and devotee
Once the green is harvested, the thick roots
Are planted in fertile soil and covered
With raised lid and dark cloth, so that shoots
Turn white while being fed and mothered
From that darkness spring white, soft, bitter spikes
That have the bitter sweetness that I like

The First Seconds

Ah, these few first seconds of the day when
Your gross body has not sunk into the
dream body yet and dreams still linger, then
a yawn strikes and sets silken darkness free
Eyelids flutter in vain; light's still too strong
Arms move upwards, cradling your sleepy head
Reluctantly, you rejoin, you prolong
that moment in bed when awareness spreads
slowly, and your blood wakes your weary bones
your floppy muscles, your sluggish ass
While your throat moans and your chest groans
And your tongue wets your soft lips. Ah alas
You must join the marching band named "daytime"
I know it feels like a crime, but you'll be fine….

They've Gone Away

The sonnets are not announcing themselves
often any longer, they've flown away
These translucent, mysterious elves
Have decided to continue their play
elsewhere. They must have been bored with my head
I hope they find another friendly host
Someone who writes them down instead
of me. Someone who on Facebook posts
I welcomed them in like good old friends
I wave them farewell without regret
I don't pretend that they have no end
I'm just glad we momentarily met
They're fun, little puzzle parasites
who rewrite my daily joys and delights

Hundred And Fifty-Four Sonnets

Hundred and fifty-four sonnets he wrote
The emperor of sonnets: Will Shakespeare
I am too much in awe of him to quote
His senses were sharp, and his mind was clear
I have not read his handsome sonnets this year
For fear of falling flat by his dazzling light
I've navigated under my own steam
And mustered all my second language might
I may open Will's book of sonnets tonight
Because this is my last sonnet for now
I will invite the sharp bite of his light
I will again be in awe, sighing: wow
I may be tempted to jot down one more
But no, I stop at a hundred and fifty-four

ABOUT SONNETS

A sonnet is a type of poem with a specific structure, typically 14 lines, that follows a particular rhyme scheme and meter (often iambic pentameter). Sonnets originated in Italy in the 13th century and became widely popular in English literature during the Renaissance, especially through the works of poets like William Shakespeare. The two most common forms of sonnets are:

Petrarchan (or Italian) Sonnet

- Structure: Divided into an *octave* (eight lines) and a *sestet* (six lines).
- Rhyme Scheme: ABBAABBA for the octave; the sestet may vary but is often CDECDE or CDCDCD.
- Purpose: Often introduces a problem or question in the octave and offers a resolution or reflection in the sestet.

Shakespearean (or English) Sonnet

- Structure: Consists of three *quatrains* (four-line stanzas) and a final *couplet* (two lines).
- Rhyme Scheme: ABABCDCDEFEFGG.
- Purpose: Each quatrain typically explores a different aspect of the theme, with the final couplet providing a twist or concluding thought.

ABOUT SONNETS

The Key Characteristics of a Sonnet are:

- **Meter:** Sonnets are often written in iambic pentameter, which means each line has ten syllables with a rhythm of an unstressed syllable followed by a stressed syllable (da-DUM).
- **Theme:** Sonnets traditionally explore themes of love, beauty, mortality, nature, and philosophical musings.
- **Volta (or "Turn"):** Most sonnets include a "turn" or shift in perspective or argument, often occurring between the octave and sestet in Petrarchan sonnets or in the final couplet of Shakespearean sonnets.

The most famous sonnet is by Shakespeare (Sonnet 18):

Shall I compare thee to a summer's day?
Thou art more lovely and more temperate:
Rough winds do shake the darling buds of May,
And summer's lease hath all too short a date.

Sometime too hot the eye of heaven shines,
And often is his gold complexion dimmed;
And every fair from fair sometime declines,
By chance or nature's changing course untrimmed;

But thy eternal summer shall not fade
Nor lose possession of that fair thou owest;
Nor shall Death brag thou wanderest in his shade,
When in eternal lines to time thou growest:

So long as men can breathe or eyes can see,
So long lives this, and this gives life to thee.

ABOUT THE AUTHOR

Suzanne Visser

Suzanne Visser LLM (1957) began her writing career in the Netherlands. She published through several good publishing houses such as Atlas, Leopold and Bert Bakker.

Her novel *De Vismoorden;* The Fish Murders, was translated into French, German, and Spanish. Clear Mind Press has published this successful book in English.

Visser has lived in Australia since 2000. She now writes in English and is a versatile and productive writer.

Bibliography

Short stories: De pracht van het dagelijks leven; 1991, Bert Bakker

Thriller: De Vismoorden; Atlas Uitgeverij, 2000

published in German as Das Japanische Rätsel, DVA, 2001

in French as Les Meurtres au Poisson, Noir sur Blanc, 2002

in Spanish as Sushi, Ediciones B., 2003

in English as The Fish Murders, Clear Mind Press, 2022

Children's book: De Verdwijning, Leopold, 2005

Novel: Terra Nostra, Bookhost, 2003

Novel: Een man met mooie benen, Mistral, 2006

Non-fiction: I, Unborn, Undying (a Search for the Self), For a Clear Mind, 2016

Non-fiction: The Elephant's Tooth, Crime in Alice Springs, Clear Mind Press 2022

The Elephant's Tooth, Crime in Rural Australia, Clear Mind Press 2022

Non-fiction: Marks on Paper, Essays on drawing, seeing and looking, Clear Mind Press 2023

Non-fiction: Never Retire, an exploration of old age, Clear Mind Press 2023

Novella: Cash, 2024

Poetry: Hundred and Fifty Four Sonnets, 2024

ABOUT THE AUTHOR

https://www.clearmindpress.com/suzanne-visser

Clear Mind Press
https://www.clearmindpress.com/

Hundred and Fifty Four Sonnets

© Suzanne Visser

Published by Clear Mind Press, 2024

Alice Springs, Australia

ISBN Print: 9780645888768

Ebook; 9780645888775

Cover design: Suzanne Visser

Portrait of the author: Hazel Blake

Cover photo: Sandid on Pixabay

All rights reserved. Except as permitted under the Australian Copyright Act 1968 (for example, fair dealing for study, research, criticism or review), no part of this book may be reproduced, stored in a retrieval system, communicated or transmitted in any form or by any means without prior written permission.

All inquiries should be made to the publisher: info@clearmindpress.com

https://www.clearmindpress.com

www.ingramcontent.com/pod-product-compliance
Lightning Source LLC
Chambersburg PA
CBHW051435290426
44109CB00016B/1569